CONTENTS

❀ ❀ ❀ ❀ ❀ ❀ ❀ ❀

FOREWARD

Since the Bible declares that children are our heritage from the Lord, we need to gain all the knowledge we can concerning how properly to maintain and mature our children.

Kathie Walter's deals with several Biblical principles and life experiences in properly raising children. Her principles are Bible based and are proven in her experiences with her children. We used these principles with our three children. They have served God all their lives and are in the ministry with us today. Our children are raising our ten grand-children the same way and are gaining the same positive results.

David and Kathie have conducted several children's ministries at our Christian International seminars. They have proven that children receive the same Christ and Holy Spirit gifts and graces when they are born again and Spirit filled. They also can manifest them as well. Nothing can establish Christian children in their faith and zeal for the Lord than personally experiencing and ministering the supernatural gifts and graces of God.

David and Kathie Walters's ministry have proven to be a great blessing to the children of the church. We encourage you to receive the principles and practices presented in this book with faith and willingness. You and your children will benefit greatly.

Dr. Bill and Evelyn Hamon are founders of Christian International. Dr. Hamon is Bishop, Overseer and President. He is the author of the following books. <u>The Eternal Church, Prophets and Personal Prophecy, Prophets and the Prophetic Movement, Prophets, Pitfalls and Principles, Fulfilling your Personal Prophecy.</u> Evelyn Hamon is the author of <u>The Spiritual Seasons of Life.</u>

Dr. Bill and Evelyn Hamon

PARENTING

— BY THE
SPIRIT

Published by
GOOD NEWS FELLOWSHIP MINISTRIES
220 Sleepy Creek Rd.
Macon, GA. 31210
Phone: (478) 757-8071
Fax: (478) 757-0136
e-mail: goodnews@reynoldscable.net
http://www.goodnews.netministries.org

Good News Fellowship Ministries
220 Sleepy Creek Road
Macon Georgia 31210

Unless otherwise noted, all Scripture quotations are
from the New King James Version of the Bible.

✿✿✿✿✿✿✿✿✿✿✿✿✿✿✿✿✿✿✿✿✿✿✿✿✿✿✿✿✿✿✿✿✿✿✿

DEDICATION

**This book is dedicated of course to my own family.
Without them, it's obvious that there would be no book.**

**Secondly, to all the honest young moms who came and said
"I love my kids, but sometimes they drive me crazy!"**

**Thirdly, to Cathy Seats and her family.
Without her I would have gotten nowhere fast.**

Thanks everyone. ❤

The Godly Seed Under Attack

Because of the sin of Adam and Eve, conflict arose between the seed of the women and the seed of the serpent. This caused a change in relationship between people and snakes. The result of this was strife. *"And I will put enmity between you and the woman, and between your seed and her seed; He shall bruise your head, and you shall bruise His heel."* (**Gen.3:15**). This conflict is not just between humans and venomous snakes, but more importantly, between the **ungodly seed** and the **godly seed.**

We have a picture in the Old Testament of Pharaoh attempting to kill the sons of the Hebrews. *"So Pharaoh commanded all his people saying, "Every son who is born you shall cast into the river"* (**Ex.1:22**). The King of Egypt's reason for killing the Hebrew male children was the fear of their increase of strength and power. Although the Hebrews were suffering under Egyptian bondage, God was still blessing their crops, their livestock, and the fruit of their loins. As Satan entered the serpent in the garden to war against the godly seed, he also entered Pharaoh to destroy the Hebrew seed, for he knew that there was going to come a **"deliverer,"** which was Moses. Fortunately Moses's parents did not bow to Pharaoh's command, but hid him for three months, because they were not afraid of the King's command, and they saw he was a beautiful child. (**See Heb.11:23**).

God gave them back their son to nurse him, after he was discovered by Pharaoh's daughter. His biological mother breast fed him for the first two or three years of his life. During that time she also instilled enough of the Hebrew faith into him, so that he could fulfil his destiny.

"By faith Moses, when he became of age refused to be called the son of Pharaoh's daughter," **(Heb.11.24).** He was raised and educated, (and remember, some of those educators would have been magicians) in Pharaoh's court, yet he never abandoned his faith. His parents did not sacrifice Moses to the spirit of the age. Neither must we sacrifice our seed to the spirit of this age. (Peer pressure, today's moral value system, humanistic philosophy, etc). *"Train up a child in the way that he should go, and when he is old he will not depart from it."* **(Prov.22:6).** How are our children coping when they are exposed to the public school system, and have friends who do not know the Lord?

In the book of Matthew we read *"Then Herod, when he saw that he was deceived by the wise men, was exceedingly angry; and he sent forth and put to death all the male children who were in Bethlehem and in all it's districts, from two years old and under, according to the time which he had determined from the wise men."* **(Matt.2:16.)** Although Herod did not want any competition, Satan was using him to try to destroy Jesus (the Godly seed) for he knew He was to be the people's **"deliverer."** We thank God that the wise men were spiritual enough to believe in dreams and visions? For they were warned in a dream not to return to Herod and tell him the whereabouts of the Holy Child. The parents of Jesus were also people who believed that God spoke supernaturally, through angels and dreams. They heeded the angelic warning and hid until after Herod's death, thus enabling Jesus Christ to fulfil His destiny. Are we spirit led when parenting our children? A few moral objects lessons and some religious stories will teach them **about** God, but they need to **know** God for themselves. They need to be taught by example, to walk in the realm of the Spirit.

The scriptures teach us that the Church is part of the godly remnant that will be saved. **(Compare Rom.9:24-26. / Rom.9:27.**

/ **Rom.11:17-24).** When Jesus Christ rose from the dead he became the first born among many brethren. **(See Rom.8:29).** We have many sons of God at war with the sons of Satan. In Romans nine we read " . . .*Unless the Lord of Sabboath had left us a seed, We would have become like Sodom, and we would have been made like Gomorrah. "***(Rom.9:29).** Many western countries including America and the U.K., are fast becoming like Sodom and Gomorrah, because Satan is out to destroy the godly seed. The Church contains that seed. Our children are called to be the deliverers. This end-time generation is destined by God to come forth as "Warriors", Dragon-Slayers" and Champions" to disciple the nations, in these last days. Satan knows only too well, the anointing that is waiting for these young people. This last great end-time army will consist of many children and teens. Satan's plan is to seduce our children into leaving God's Army, turning traitor and joining his camp. He failed to destroy Moses. He failed to destroy Jesus. He **must** fail to destroy our children. *"The Spirit of the Lord is upon Me, because He has anointed Me to preach the gospel to the poor. He has sent Me to heal the brokenhearted, to preach deliverance to the captives, and recovery of sight to the blind. To set at liberty those who are oppressed. To preach the acceptable year of the Lord. "* **(Luk.4:18).** If satan can anoint youngsters in the rock music world to preach their gospel of drugs, sex and rebellion, (which are taking thousands of youngsters into hell), cannot the Holy Spirit anoint **our** children, (the godly seed) to bring even more souls into the kingdom?

CURSES AND BLESSINGS.

As satan was successful in polluting our original parents (Adam and Eve) he has tried to keep that pollution going down through history. *"You shall not bow down to them nor serve them (the spirit of the age) for I the Lord your God am a jealous God, visiting the iniquity of the fathers upon the children to the third and fourth generations of those that hate me. "* **(Deut.5:9).** As we have

7

inherited genes from our parents, our children usually have similar physical traits as us. They also tend to inherit some of our flaws and weaknesses. There are generational curses that can come upon our children and us. Stubbornness, rebellion, immorality, drunkenness, etc. can be passed down from generation to generation.

"Cursed is everyone who does not continue in all the things which are written in the book of the law to do them" **(Gal.3:10).**

Many church children have a religious upbringing without the reality. They attempt to keep certain rules, laws and commandments and **continually fail.** They are trying to be Christians without the power of the Holy Spirit, and that keeps them under the curse.

When they become real Christians, the curse is removed, for Jesus was cursed for them, and they are free to inherit the blessings of redemption. *"Christ has redeemed us from the curse of the law, having become a curse for us . . ."* **(Gal.3:13).** *"That the blessings of Abraham might come upon the Gentiles in Christ Jesus, that we might receive the promise of the Spirit through faith."* **(Gal.3:14).** *"Then Peter said to them, Repent, and let every one of you be baptized in name of Jesus Christ for remission of sins, and you shall receive the gift of the Holy Spirit. For the promise is to you and to your children, ..."* **(Acts.2:38-39).** As we and they appropriate the promise of the Spirit we can inherit the blessings. As curses can be passed on down through generations, so blessings also can be passed down.

A newspaper story told of two families. One was the family of a well-known atheist. The other was the family of Jonathan Edwards, the great American preacher. They were contemporaries. The atheist married a godless wife, and from this union to the fourth generation, of 1200 descendants, there were 400 who were physical self wrecks, 310 paupers, 150 criminals and 7 murderers - and that was in an age that was considered puritanical.

Jonathan Edwards married a godly woman. Of 1394 known descendants to the fourth generation there were 14 college and university presidents, 100 professors, 100 ministers of the Gospel, missionaries and theological teachers; More than 100 judges and lawyers; 60 physicians, authors and editors - and almost every North American industry has been influenced by an offspring of Jonathan Edwards.

The bible, has given us many promises regarding our children here are a some of them. *"The seed of the righteous shall be delivered."*(**Prov.11:21**) *"I will pour My Spirit upon their seed, and My blessings upon thy offspring."*(**Isa.44:3**). *"But thus saith the Lord, Even the captives of the mighty shall be taken away, and the prey of the terrible shall be delivered: for I will contend with him that contendeth with thee, and I will save **thy children**."*(**Isa.49:25**) *"And all **thy children** shall be taught of the Lord; and great shall be the peace of **thy children**."* (**Isa.54:13**)

"My Spirit is upon thee, and My words which I have put in thy mouth, shall not depart out of thy mouth, nor out of the mouth of thy seed, nor out of the mouth of thy seed's seed, (grandchildren) saith the Lord, from henceforth and for ever." (**Isa.59:21**)

"Believe on the Lord Jesus Christ and thou shalt be saved and thy house."(**Acts.16:31**)

In the remainder of this book Kathie shares some insights and keys that will enable you to raise your children to be children of destiny.

David Walters

From the "Armor of God" *childrens bible study*

INTRODUCTION

The GodSquad

For several years I have observed young parents struggling with their children. This prompted a desire in me to help them. Many mothers looked frantic, frustrated and "frazzled," as they tried to cope with unruly youngsters. It is not uncommon today to see children of all ages running about unrestrained in stores, restaurants and churches. The poor parents are embarrassed and confused, as their words of correction fall to the ground. My heart goes out to them.

If you as a Christian parent have a burden for your children to be anointed and to stand strong in these last days, and if you want to see them taking their place in this great end-time army that God is now raising up, then I do believe that I can be of some help. Am I writing as an expert in parenting? Not at all, there are many parents who are greater sources of inspiration than me. Yet, I do have the help and expertise of the Holy Spirit to guide and direct me in raising my children for the Lord. I have seen some, (but not many) "almost perfect" mothers. They appear to have "almost perfect" little kids. Most of these angelic like children are like mini adults, they have Jesus in their heart, and they are very polite. Many of them are real sweet, but are they on fire for God? It depends what you want. If it's just a good, respectable, agreeable, honest and proper offspring, then I can't help you too much. But, if you have a burden for your children to be anointed and strong in the power of God, then I do believe that the Holy Spirit has given me a few keys. The behavior and characteristics of Christ will be manifested in their lives, because they are getting to know the Lord and learning to love Him.**(See Matt 6:33)**

From "Being A Christian" *childrens bible study*

— Chapter One —

The Equipment

If you are **serious** about your children, you must learn to serve the Lord and live in the anointing. If you want them to put God first all the days of their lives then please don't attempt to do what I say without making this check list yourself. You are going to need **spiritual** authority, so it is important that you get to know the Holy Spirit very well. You can't have spiritual authority if all you are living in is a form of religion, without any real power.

Let me take a few moments to talk about the Holy Spirit. I love Him dearly, He is wonderful. His job is to make manifest everything that we believe. In other words, if you believe that God **loves** you, the Holy Spirit is there to make sure that you **experience** that love. Wouldn't it be pitiful if we had a conversation with Jesus that went something like this?

JESUS — "Now, you are saved, and you are going to heaven, meanwhile I've left you an inheritance to consume your lives."

US — "How wonderful, Lord what is it?."

JESUS — "I am going to give you a whole lot of religious information, and you can learn all kinds of doctrines and quote lots of scriptures." I had that revelation myself for six years and then decided it was too hard. While I was still single I ran away to Australia and decided to give up trying to live the Christian life. Some friends continued to pray for me, and two years later God gave me an experience to show me that He was not a doctrine, but a wonderful **person.**

The Holy Spirit wants to fellowship with you and **He** wants you to love Him and know Him. He is always present. He cares about your children even more than you do. Learn to love Him for yourself, and listen to His voice, He will be more than happy to equip you to raise your children to fulfil their calling.

It will be hard for your children to love the Holy Spirit, if **you** don't, so the ball is in your court. The Christian life is not difficult and boring. It is exciting and adventurous, because it is supernatural.

Perhaps you have lost your joy, forgotten God's wonderful grace, and entered into a works mentality. If that's true then you must get out of it. Be simple, ask the Holy Spirit to show you how to return to your first love. Fall in love with Jesus again, and enjoy your relationship with Him. My children are accustomed to me experiencing the Holy Spirit's anointing of laughter or intercession. They don't think God is religious, they know He is real. They have also had many experiences for themselves of the power of the Holy Spirit.

Are you being bogged down with the cares of the world? Jesus said, *"Take no thought of what you shall eat, or what shall you wear, for your Heavenly Father knows you have need of these things."* **(Matt.6:31-32.)** *"No one engaged in warfare entangles himself with affairs of this life, that he may please Him who enlisted him as a soldier."* **(2.Tim.2:4).** Take a moment and ask yourself, "What is my life all about?" Is most of your time and energy spent in making a living? Are you largely consumed by sports or some other activity? If so, you will have lost your fire and excitement. You don't want your children to get the impression that God is reserved for Sundays, for when you become concerned about their spiritual lives, they won't understand why. After all if your spiritual life doesn't seem that important to you, why should theirs? Remember God has a destiny for you to fulfill as an individual and as a family.

Every desire buried deep within can only be met in the destiny that God has planned for you. That is why there are so many

14

Christians who are still unfulfilled and boring. You must be determined enough to "push through the crowd" and find the path which was prepared for you before the foundation of the world.**(See Mark 5:27)**

The reason I am asking you these questions is, you cannot give what you haven't got yourself. It is very difficult for a child to stay on fire for God, if the parents arc full of compromises. In these days Satan is out to capture our youngsters. He'll use anything or everything to get their attention. They want excitement and a reason for living. They need a sense of purpose and only the reality, the power, and the plan of God can give them that. You can tell when people don't feel relevant, we have seen many youngsters who don't feel they are important to God or anyone else. They know mama loves them, but as far as any real sense of purpose in this world, it is not in their thinking. This is a wonderful time to be alive. There is a great move of God coming, we are seeing the stirring's of it and it is exciting. This younger generation has a mighty call on their lives. God is raising an army of young people who will be anointed, appointed and sent. They will disciple the nations and reap the harvest. They will see great signs and wonders, as God confirms the Gospel. The devil would like your son or daughter in **his** army. Don't think your child is too young to be trained for God. Satan doesn't think they are to young to be infiltrated by his demonic powers. He even kills many of them before they are born, through his abortion program.

Tiny tots can be in need of deliverance because of occult toys and cartoons. We have witnessed very small children experiencing deliverance from demonic activity. The Holy Spirit can also minister to and through children. We have also seen children caught up in the Spirit for several hours, with a spirit of intercession, weeping for others, confessing their sins, and asking God to move on nations. We have also witnessed many healing's and miracle's through young people as they have prayed for the sick.

In our meetings the Holy Spirit often comes powerfully upon

large numbers of children, including teens. Many have visions, prophecies, and words of knowledge. God can minister to and through any age of child, if there are no barriers.

My husband, David had a vision a few years ago, he saw armies of young people in many nations. They had guns and other weapons. In preparation they were undergoing training for war. Then the Holy Spirit showed him young people in America, they were goofing around, aimless and not caring. The Lord spoke to him and said, *"Satan is preparing his army, and My Church is entertaining her children."*

David now spends his life stirring up church leaders and parents to get their children anointed and ready for the move of God. They can't do it without your co-operation Mom and Dad, you must get the vision. If you have been lukewarm, and backslidden in your heart - I pray, that you are convicted by the Holy Spirit. Remember, this is a serious hour that we are living in. There is not time to play religious games.

"Dear Lord Jesus,
I thank you so much for all the wonderful miracles that you did at camp, especially the lady with the ear, but please don't let Johnny come next year" Megan, age 8.

— Chapter Two —

The Resolution or the Wish

When I was a child, I was not what one would term a good little girl. I was extremely selfish, jealous, very strong willed, and spoilt. I usually got my way, not that my parents didn't try, but I was too strong for them to cope with. I would wear them out with my insistence. They loved me, and gave in, it was easier than fighting me. I learned that if I didn't take **"No"** for an answer, they eventually gave me whatever I wanted. There were no Christians in our family that we were aware of. Somewhere, there was an old aunt in a nursing home, who occasionally wrote us letters about God. My parents put it down to her old age, They thought she was just getting senile.

I heard the Gospel message when I was twenty years old. I knew it was the truth, and made a commitment to Christ when I met David. He was the one who witnessed to me and I was saved through his testimony. But I needed deliverance, and no one around at that time could help me. After a few years of trying and failing, I decided that there was no way I could live the Christian Life. Having an opportunity to go to Australia with a friend, I saw it as a chance to escape from the well-meaning Christians around me. After a couple of years of worldliness, I had a visitation from the Lord. The Holy Spirit fell upon me in the office where I was then working. The love of God was overwhelming I wept and wept. No-one knew what was wrong with me, and so they put into a taxi and sent me home. I spent the rest of the day finding my way back to God. Although at the time

I knew nothing of the things of the Spirit, I did have an experience, the presence of God was strongly manifested. After that day, every person I witnessed to got saved. In a short time, there was a good-sized group of people meeting to study the Bible and pray. I knew that I was not really called to Australia. I went back to England and married David a few weeks later. Because of the experience I had in Sydney, I knew there was something more to the Christian life than I had been originally presented with. I was hungry for a deeper relationship with God, and so David and myself accompanied with a small group of friends began to meet to pray and seek the Lord together. We were all filled with the Holy Spirit a short while later. After that EVERYTHING changed. Our whole lives were totally different. I was delivered from the demonic spirits that had hindered me for so long. The Holy Spirit untangled the mess I was in inside, and graced us with a wonderful revival in the South of London.

I greatly desired to have an intimate relationship with the Holy Spirit and so He met me and taught me many wonderful things. The most important was that the realm of the supernatural was my **inheritance**. I learned that there was no situation that the Holy Spirit did not understand or know about, and so His wisdom was awesome and available to me. One thing I was sure of, I knew that allowing children to have their way, only made them confused and miserable. I did whatever I wanted and some of those things were really stupid. I remember once climbing into the coffins in the pyramids of Egypt, I thought it was "fun." These kinds of escapades had brought about my need for some serious deliverance.

I realized that I was going to have to make a resolution, when my daughter Faith was born in 1977. "Wishing" was not going to make a dent in any problems that might arise. We determined that Faith was not going to rule our home, our lives, or even her life. We believed that God had called us to the ministry and that there was also a call on her life. So she was going to be raised with that in mind. We knew that she was more God's than ours, we were just caretakers. We let her know that from the time she could understand words.

Everyone is called to some kind of ministry, even if you have a full time job. Seek the Lord earnestly and ask Him to tell you about His call on the life of your child. Believe Him. When we have needed a word from the Lord, I have always asked Him to speak very specifically. Usually through someone who does not know about the present situation. That way I've known it was really from God and not someone's opinion. There is no point making your child spend years learning Spanish, if his call is to Russia or Africa. He could have spent that time doing something that would enable him to fulfill his calling.

"Dear Heavenly Father,
    Thanks for all the missionaries and Sunday school teachers. And thanks for all the miracles that you do. I would be very pleased if you would heal my bicycle". Tim, age 6.

Cover picture from "Armor of God" *childrens bible study*

Chapter Three

The "Nitty-Gritty"

When babies are first born, there isn't usually too much of a battle. They cry when they are hungry or uncomfortable. Normally they don't fight with you about what to wear or what to eat, although the first attempt at manipulation sometimes comes from the crib. A few months after the birth of Faith I realized that the beautiful baby with the great big smile, began to take note of a few things. When she cried someone came and picked her up. It didn't take long for her to learn to "cry" whenever she wanted up. Sometimes that was fine, but it can become a very demanding situation. If you are not careful it can start to rule your day (and night).

This whole thing is really about control. The child, if not brought under proper discipline will rule you, and dominate your home and your life.

We were in another country last year and were invited out to dinner by a wealthy young couple. They brought along their four children. The fancy restaurant turned into a zoo. Those children were all over the place. Climbing across the table, running to other people's tables, and yelling and shouting. Gradually everyone else left the restaurant and we were the only diners there. Even the table servers took those little kids and walked them around **outside.** Eventually the young woman spoke to me as the boy was shrieking at the top of his lungs. "He wants an ice cream," she stated. "I think he wants a hand on his bottom," I said. She was very upset with me and hardly spoke to me again. At that point I didn't really care whether she did or not. If the children are going to learn to obey God's voice then they must first learn to obey yours.

I realize that talking about your children is a very touchy thing. We are talking about the "apple of your eye," but if you truly love your youngsters, the safest thing in the whole world for them is to know God and listen to **His** voice. *"He is our (and their) strong tower and place of safety."* (**Ps.61:3**).

The first real incident I remember with Faith was when she was about five months old. I often gave her some mashed banana, but one day I tried some peach flavored baby food. She spat it out, and I gave her a little more, she spat it out again and once more I put a little into her mouth. She looked me right in the eye and **pretended** to throw up. I couldn't believe it! There was no doubt that she was pretending. I went into a mild shock. Here was this innocent baby trying to **manipulate** me. At that point I realized something very important, this manipulation was an instinct, she didn't have to learn how to do it. Mom, the sooner you realize this the better off you will be.

We gave Faith plenty of love and affection and attention, but we tried to show her that it didn't come on demand. I started to get her out of the crib the same time every morning. At first she would cry for me to come and get her earlier. I would go and check that she was O.K. even give her a kiss, but I didn't get her out until it was the time. I had some things to do, for a start I wanted to spend a little time with the Lord by myself before the day got rolling. Faith very quickly adapted to it. She would wake up and sit and play with a couple of toys until I fetched her. I soon learned to tell if there was a real need, or if it was just a whine. It is interesting that today at seventeen years old, Faith has an extraordinary amount of patience.

Neither Faith and Lisa ever disturbed our guests when they were staying in our home. They read, or played quietly until the adults were up and moving around. They never came to our room unless there was something urgent, and they always knocked first. They still do. When I first brought Faith home from the hospital, she woke up about three times in the night to be fed. I felt happy to do this for a couple of months. One day I felt the Holy Spirit tell me it wasn't necessary. So the next night when the second feed time came and Faith cried, I went and patted her, but I didn't get her up. She continued to cry and it was very hard to stay where I was, but eventually she fell asleep. The next night and the third night the same thing happened, although she didn't cry for so long, after that she never woke up for that middle feed. A few months later I decided to cut another one. I asked my doctor about it to make sure I was on the right track. He told me that our bodies quickly become like internal clocks. They tend to control us because of habit, but they are not always necessary. Before I put Faith to bed I began to give her something a little more satisfying, like a banana. It prevented her from having an empty feeling in the night, and so she slept longer. Very soon she slept all through the night. It is not right that a small child should rule the house from morning until evening. Make a proper bedtime and stick to it. You and your spouse need some child-free time in the evening. A number of young parents seem to have a real problem putting their children to bed. Many little ones will scream and cry until you allow them up again, or they eventually go to bed more out of exhaustion than anything else. It makes for a very miserable child. If your child does that, go back and say, "No." Explain that if you do have to return to the room it will be to give some discipline. If you have to go again, keep your word, a little bop on the bottom will do fine. **Don't** give in, remain pleasant, but firm. After a few evenings, you will not have a problem. I spoke with a grade school teacher a while ago, she said she could spot the children who fell asleep in front of the television every night. They had a problem concentrating and didn't learn all they could.

— Chapter Four —

Spiritual Authority

If you try to take control outside of the Holy Spirit you will get into some head-on clashes. You will be worn out, and the children will be full of strife and aggression (so will you). Eventually you will be tempted to give up. So now is the time to determine what you want for your child. If you decide you are raising him or her for the call of God, you will have confidence, because you know the Holy Spirit wants the same thing as you. He will help you minister to your children.

When you have to discipline your children tell them constantly how much God loves them. Tell them He wants them to be saved and to know Jesus and tell them about the great plan that He has for their lives. Tell about the great anointing they will come into as they give their lives to Him. Let them know they were ordained by God, before the foundation of the world, they have a place that no one else in the whole world can fill. A great destiny, what a privilege, what a special person they are. Never stop telling them, it will keep them from sin. One day Faith was invited to the home of a friend, the girl's mother was upstairs and the girl found one of her fathers video's under the bookcase. She put it in the video player and found it was a X-Rated movie. Faith left and came home. "Mom," she said, "I couldn't watch it, all I could hear was your voice telling me that God has an awesome destiny for my life."

NEVER YIELD TO DISOBEDIENCE

God wants us all to learn INSTANT obedience. One day it may be a matter of life or death. A friend of mine in England took her little boy Daniel out shopping. In one store there were some stairs at the back. While his mother was busy looking at some merchandise, the boy disappeared. The only place to go was up those stairs. My friend followed and found Daniel on the roof of the building. He was very near the edge. Instead of screaming, she softly called his name. "Daniel, come here to me." He didn't hesitate, but turned and come right back to her arms. What a good thing that he had learned instant obedience. There are some things that you can explain if you like, but don't feel you have to explain every command, they must learn to trust you when you tell them to do something. At some point in your life, your **instant** obedience to God's voice could be the most important action you ever took.

A few years ago, I was driving a car in England. I was travelling at a good speed, as it was a main highway. The Holy Spirit suddenly spoke to me. He told me to put my foot on the brake. I didn't, as I could see no reason. Again He said, "Put your foot on the brake." This time I pressed down gently and then harder. **There was no brake,** the car kept on going. I took my foot off the accelerator. As the car slowed, I changed down through the gears and let the vehicle come to a halt. The last few yards I pulled into a gas station that just "happened" to be there! A quarter of a mile further down the road was a main junction! I don't like to think about what could have happened, if I reached the junction with no brakes.

Another time I was driving my car in Orlando, Florida. I came toward a railway crossing. The Holy Spirit spoke to me. "Stop," He said. I stopped immediately, just before the crossing. I didn't understand why, the gate was not down and the light was not flashing. I had the radio on and so I didn't hear any train. As I stopped the car, a train went straight through in front of me!

From "The Fruit of the Spirit" *childrens bible study*

26

Chapter Five

Battle of the Will

In rearing your children there will be an occasional battle of the will, but you must keep your authority. One day Faith was sitting in her high chair. I had given her some carrots to eat for lunch. She decided she didn't want them, she wanted a cookie. I told her to eat them. She wouldn't. After a while she wanted out of the high chair. I told her she would get out of the chair when she had eaten the carrots. Faith pushed them further away, so I left her in the high chair and did a few things nearby in the way of housework. She cried. I came and pushed the carrots back to the front of the tray, then continued with the housework. She knew the carrots were still the issue. After a while she screamed and sobbed. I returned and comforted her and told her she was sweet and lovely, but I left her in the high chair. I couldn't believe that a sweet little girl could be so stubborn. She stayed in the high chair for almost four hours. I got her out once to change her, but I put her right back with the carrots. Faith finally ate them and I put her bed exhausted, but the next day she was in the sweetest mood I ever saw. She was also very loving to me. She felt safe because she had real boundaries and inwardly she was relieved that they were there, incidentally she now likes carrots.

One other major battle was when we were in a store. Faith was seated in the cart. She saw another little girl running around between the clothes. The little child was pulling things off the shelves and grabbing anything she could get her hands on. Faith must have thought it was fun, because she wanted to join in. I said, "No," but she whined (whining is definitely not allowed) I gave a light tap on her hands, but she got more defiant. Then she cried and then yelled. I decided to leave the store rather than ruin everyone's shopping time. When I put her down near the front of the store, she attempted to run back. I caught her dress and pulled her back. She now realized she was in trouble anyway, so she would make a last desperate attempt at getting her way. She then pitched herself on the floor and threw a tantrum. As I looked down at her, I didn't get angry, but my spirit rose up inside me. I determined right then that it would **never** happen again. I picked her up, put her in the car and drove home. When we went inside the house she was still screaming. I think she was scared to stop at this point. I put her in the crib and left the room. She continued, but she wore herself out and fell asleep. She awoke and was whimpering. When I went into the room she put her arms out to me, a bit of it was real, but mostly she was trying to ward off the inevitable. I was tempted to let it pass, but my spirit was disturbed. I let her see that I was concerned about what had happened. I sat her down, and told her that this was never going to happen again. NEVER NEVER **NEVER!** She was alarmed, but it is dangerous to let a child get out of control. The demonic forces love it, they are around to see if they can get in on the act. I gave her a spanking, and made her stay in her room for the rest of the day. She was a very sociable child. It was a great punishment to her to hear us talking and laughing, and not be able to be part of it. Faith never ever threw a tempter tantrum again.

Never Never - no no

I trusted the Holy Spirit, and when He moved in my heart, I acted. Faith was just learning to talk and one day when I told her to do something she said, "No." I told her again and she said, "No." I said, "Yes" and she said, "No, no." Each time she said the word, "No" I noticed that she got a little stronger in her emphasis.

It bothered me, so I prayed about it. The Lord told me this. It is not necessary that the word, "No" be a part of a child's vocabulary in responding to their parents. He told me not to allow her to use that word to me or anyone in authority over her. There are two exceptions, "No, thank you" and, "No, Sir/Ma'am," if it is in response to a question. But, "No" in the way of answering a request is not at all acceptable. Of course, "No" should be used in answer to an invitation to do something ungodly. To this day, I have never heard her say it. There is a defiance that comes with the use of the word, so don't allow it in your house. Sometimes Faith or Lisa have said things like, "Do I have to," but we quickly tell them that what we say is not open for discussion.

Sometimes I have made a quick decision and afterward have felt that my first decision wasn't the right one. Faith and Lisa know if they don't "bug" us, the Lord will tell us, if we need to reverse a decision. One example was when Faith wanted to use some of our frequent flyer miles to get an air ticket to spend a few weeks with a girl friend in Indiana. At first we said, "No," and Faith said, "O.K.," but a few days later, I felt the Holy Spirit moving on me to change my mind. I told Faith that the Lord gave me the green light and would not only get her ticket, but make sure she had enough pocket money to have a good time while she was away. I don't pretend to be always right, if I am wrong, I usually own up.

Dear God,
*   I have never been in a church like this one I was at today. Those people were so noisy, but I liked it in the end, it was better than the ball-game."*

29

— Chapter Six —

Asking First

I have visited many people in their homes who have small children, and some not so small. Their houses are almost barren. Maybe because I am English I like to have china, lace and little pieces of porcelain around the house. In many homes I have felt sad, because the parents have told me, "We can't have anything nice, because the children will grab it and break it. We don't buy good furniture and we have locked away all our vases and ornaments." I have lots of "things" and I have never moved a vase or ornament from where it was originally placed. I thought about the problem and sought the Holy Spirit. Sometimes I would be alarmed when friends would bring their children to my home, because they would take off running through the house, grabbing my stuff even barging into my bedroom.

I sat and watched one mother who was in my home. The woman was trying to talk to me about something important, but it was impossible. Her children ran all over the place, grabbing everything that caught their eye. The poor woman spent all her time chasing them, begging them to behave, pleading with them to leave things alone. She became so distraught and frantic and I felt so sorry for her. It was as though she was talking to them and yelling at them, knowing full well that they were not going to take the slightest notice. What a shame!

This is what the Holy Spirit showed me concerning this kind of situation. At home, Faith and Lisa had their toys and books in their bedroom. Outside their room, there were other people to consider. I would tell them that anyone else's stuff, including mine, was **not to be touched under any circumstances.** In the den I kept a basket of toys that they could take out and play with. I had a coffee table clear for them to use. I kept a large recliner they could climb in etc. I used the same principle when we visited someone else's home. I took a few of their toys with us. I taught them to **ask** permission before they could touch or pick up certain things in the house. They stayed with me unless someone told them they could go into another room etc. I reminded them of how they had felt, when other children had gone into their room and taken their belongings without asking. I cannot remember ever being embarrassed by their behavior. Lest I should give the impression that my kids were faultless, I want to let you know that they did get up to some mischief. Faith unwound toilet rolls all over the place, she always wanted to see how far they would stretch through the house (any house).

"Dear Jesus,

You are very kind to all the poor people and the people suffering in poor countries. Do you ever run out of money? Is there a bank up there?" Tina, age 5.

From "The Fruit of the Spirit" *childrens bible study*

Chapter Seven

Screaming and Whining

Some behavior patterns can open the children up to strong self will and even demonic spirits, if allowed to go unchecked. One of those areas is screaming. When a child is allowed to scream, they are not in control of themselves, and out of your control. It is very important that you are living under the anointing and the discipline of the Holy Spirit. This way you have authority **in the Holy Spirit.** This authority protects them from the snares and traps of the enemy. If you don't think the devil has an interest in them, then think again. He has heard those things that have been spoken over your children and knows that potentially they can become mighty for God. I try to fellowship with the Holy Spirit always, and there have been many occasions when He has revealed things to me that I could not have known through my natural thoughts.

Often I hear children fighting and screaming. I never allowed Faith or Lisa to scream, not in a fight, not even when I had to spank them. The Holy Spirit said that it was unnecessary.

SELF-CONTROL

I tried to teach them to **think**, and not panic. I attempted to cover all the bases. When we were in large stores, I made sure they knew what to do if they should ever get separated from me. I told them to stand still and call my name **loudly,** this way I could hear and come and find them. What has this to do with screaming? You may ask. Well it has to do with keeping themselves under control. If you lose control, you can't think properly and sometimes it is extremely important for a child to **think.** We lost Lisa one time at the big Orlando International Airport, when she was only six. We looked around, there were so many people, it was impossible to find her. We prayed and were about to make our way to the security office. A message came over the relay system, "Would David Joy come to the Delta counter." We knew it was us that they were calling for. When we got to the counter, there was Lisa, not in the least disturbed. Later she told us that when she couldn't find us she prayed, and the Holy Spirit told her to stand still and watch for someone with a uniform. She saw a pilot and told him she was lost. He took her to the Delta counter. When they asked her name she said, "Lisa-Joy," which is her first name. Hence the call for, "David Joy."

Lisa now fourteen is going to El Salvador this year with Teen-Mania, a radical ministry who have a heart for young people to go on the mission field. None of our family are accompanying her, but she can take care of herself in the Lord. We have some friends whose eleven year daughter felt led by the Holy Spirit to go and help a ministry in New Zealand. She raised her fare and made the trip on her own. She had no problems and they were not in the least worried. When in New Zealand she was used by the Holy Spirit in a very wonderful way. I have met parents who behave as if the Lord is out of business, they don't trust Him to take care of their kids. That doesn't mean you have to be irresponsible, you have to get a witness in your spirit. And when you do, **trust Him.** Don't let the natural mind make you chicken out. Hook them up to Jesus, then they will always have someone to ask what to do.

Another kind of screaming is the kind that has to do with anger and self-will. A child can scream to cut you off. He or she can't hear you if they're screaming, and they don't want to hear you because you are saying, "No." Some people think that if you ignore it, then it will go away, that's not so.

There is a screaming that comes from fear, and although it is not a rebellious thing, it is fully yielding to the fear. Even a child can learn the truth and trust Jesus with all things. Get them out of the screaming syndrome as soon as possible and speak the truth to them. **All fear is built on a lie, deal with the lie and the fear will die.**

Be cautious when you see your small child "running the show." If grown-ups are in the middle of a conversation, teach them to wait and not just rudely interrupt you. Teach them to say, "Excuse me?" I have often been at a dinner table and a child has dominated the whole conversation. It doesn't hurt them to sit quietly until the meal is finished. It is not hard for a child to operate in a spirit of control. If you allow them they will become very obnoxious, and when your friends learn that your children are accompanying you when you visit them, they will not respond with great joy. You must have authority in the spirit always.

WHINING

Children cry for several reasons. One is when hurt and another is when they are sad. People also cry out of sentiment and emotion. Though the things may be un-real, like movies and books. (I know that there is a weeping that comes with intercession, and when the anointing of the Lord comes upon you, but I am not dealing with those things here). There is also a crying that is purely for manipulation. When seated in a restaurant one evening with some friends, we noticed a table near us with a family which included a small boy of about three or four. He cried and whined and whined and cried. I turned to see what was going on. He wanted ice cream before he had finished his dinner. When his father said, "No!" he continued crying. He cried until he got some ice cream. Then he left his ice cream and his mother told him to finish it up. He didn't want to, so he cried and whined, until they left him alone. He then wanted to get up from the table and his father again said, "No!" Guess what happened? He cried and cried until they gave in. The little boy had the whole family well under control, he manipulated the whole dinner time with his crying.

I would have taken him outside and disciplined him, but I guess by the time they thought of that they were worn out through striving with him. The child was an unhappy little fellow. He was really looking for a boundary so that he could feel safe, but there wasn't one.

"Dear Lord God,

We have lots of stuff and my Dad has a new car. My mom says he worships it. But I want to worship you. When I get a bit bigger, I want to go to Japan and preach to the school children. Could you help me with the applications and visa forms? My Mom will give me the money." John, age 9.

Chapter Eight

The Witness of Spirit — in You

The Lord has given us His Holy Spirit, He keeps us, guides us, teaches us. He always witnesses to the truth and so it is very vital that we learn to stop and listen to that inner witness. He can save you a good deal of worry and sorrow. He knows **everything** and so He is the key to your protective place as a parent.

When my second daughter, Lisa was three years old, she already had developed a strong desire to be with people. She was willing to go anywhere with anyone who would take her. She loved to visit other people's homes. Because of her desire to be with others, she wanted very much to go to the pre-school that Faith attended three mornings a week. Up to that point I had said, "No," because I wanted her to be with me a while longer. One morning I was praying for someone on the telephone in my kitchen. I left Lisa playing with some toys in her bedroom. When I got off the phone about ten minutes later I continued doing some cleaning, but it seemed very quiet. When I checked Lisa's room, she was not there, nor was she anywhere in the house. I looked outside, but she was nowhere to be seen. My mind began to work overtime, thinking of the awful things that could have happened to her.

I made myself stand still and switch off my mind and take a note of the inner witness in my spirit. My Spirit inside was calm, He was not giving me any feeling of uneasiness. My mind was going round again and there was a tremendous struggle. Who was I going to listen to? I decided that the Holy Spirit had never let me down and so I made a commitment in my heart to believe Him. He was not telling me that anything was wrong.

I called a neighbor and we began to search the neighborhood. We didn't find Lisa, so I asked the Lord if I should call the local sheriffs office, but He said, "No." Next I telephoned David, who was meeting with a couple of elders. They prayed and one of the elders received a word from the Lord, **"Green house."** I went again through the streets in our sub-division, looking at all the houses that were any shade of green at all, or even had green trim. Still nothing. I waited again on the Holy Spirit. It was one hour later. He suddenly said, "Call the sheriff's office now." I did, and they told me that a man had called just five minutes previously. A little girl had wandered into his **greenhouse** while he was potting some plants.

The sheriff was upset with me for taking so long to call, but if I had called earlier, he would have been running around looking for her as I had. He didn't understand of course, but you see the Holy Spirit knew exactly where she was and knew the right time to call the sheriff. Isn't God so very good to us. I remember when we were in a dilemma over a situation and we were not sure which direction to take. I didn't seem able to find the right answer and was trying first this way and then another. The Lord gave me a dream. I was in a dark room, trying to find the way out, but I couldn't see. I kept running into the walls. Suddenly the Holy Spirit spoke to me to be still. I sat in the middle of the room and waited. Suddenly a light shone right on the door, I calmly got up, walked toward the door and went out. So easy and simple. We spend so much time and energy unnecessarily. If only we would learn to listen to the witness of God's Spirit within us.

Recently Lisa, was away on a mission trip for a month. She called almost every night and she was having a wonderful time. One evening a friend of mine enquired how she was doing. As I began to tell him about the trip, I felt an ache in my chest. My friend also had a Word of Knowledge. The Holy Spirit told us to pray for her as she had been hurt by someone in her group. I was unable to call her, as the house I was in did not have a phone. We did pray and two days later I had an opportunity to ask her about the heartache we had felt. The word was right, and she had been able to deal with it in the Holy Spirit.

"Dear Lord Jesus,
I am willing to go on a mission trip for you, but please can I take my dog, but not my sister because she cries." Steve, age 7

Chapter Nine

The Gifts of the Spirit
(for Parents)

As the Holy Spirit knows all things, it is very important that we keep tuned in to Him. The gifts of the spirit are really just manifestations of our "tuning in." A *"Word of knowledge"* as mentioned in 1.Cor:12, means that the Holy Spirit imparts to you His knowledge about someone or a situation that you could not know with the natural mind. This is a very valuable gift to operate in with regard to your children. Sometimes children do and say things that we cannot understand. Why does a child suddenly behave in an odd or unusual way? What is going on in their mind? The Holy Spirit can give you a word of knowledge that will free the situation.

I was visiting a friend one time. She had a little girl, Rachel, a toddler. Rachel had already been potty - trained and had done very well. Then for no apparent reason that my friend, Margaret could think of, the child suddenly refused to sit on the potty. Instead she ran away and hid somewhere. It was a very distressing and frustrating experience for Margaret and her little girl. Both were in a lot of anguish. Margaret was frustrated because Rachel just buried her head in her hands when asked about it. As I sat listening to her, the Holy Spirit suddenly gave me a word of knowledge about the situation. The grandmother when baby-sitting, would make remarks when emptying the potty. You know the kind of thing, "stinky, stinky." Now I know this may sound a little crude, but it had brought about a very bad situation that affected the child in a negative way. I told my friend, "She thinks she is doing something bad, and she is ashamed." We put it right and convinced her that using the potty was very good, and that her mother was proud that she was so grown-up.

Another friend of mine named Cathy has two children who are very well behaved. Suddenly her little daughter became rebellious in little ways. It built up over a few weeks, until finally at a meeting, the child hit out at her mother. Cathy was distressed as it was not like her little girl at all. I prayed for a while and told the Lord we needed a word of knowledge to know what was wrong. The Holy Spirit spoke to me. "She has a lot of frustration". I asked Him, what she was frustrated about. He explained to me that situations had arisen, in which the child felt she was being dealt with unfairly, but she couldn't do anything about it. When we dug a little deeper, it was a very common problem. Sometimes the kids were tired and didn't want to go visiting, or stay for a long time at a meeting. Sometimes they had already had a day full of people. Cathy, with every good intention, would say for example, "We will only stay for thirty minutes," then end up staying for several hours. The child would feel that this was unjust, but she was powerless to change the situation. The children have a sense of fairness and when it is violated, they feel insecure. Keep your word. God keeps His word and we are to be like Him. There is a scripture that says, *"Swear to your own hurt and do not change."* **(Ps.15:4).** In other words, do what you say you will do and don't change your mind. Faith one day told a friend she would go and spend the night at her home. Another friend called and invited her to go to theme park on the same day. It was hard for her not to call the first friend and make an excuse. But she was faithful to her word. Just as God is faithful to His word. This is another way to help your child be like our heavenly Father.

Another insecurity comes when your words don't really mean anything. I'm sure that you have heard this kind of one way conversation. "Johnny, don't do that, if you do it again, I'll send you to your room." Johnny takes no notice. The sentence is repeated again and **again.** Finally the parent is yelling. Johnny begins to take notice. He has learned now that *when you are yelling, you mean it.* Enough said.

I have seen two opposite situations arise regarding children when the parents are having a conversation with other adults. One is that the parents will not allow the children to speak a word. One small boy wanted to go the rest-room, but his mother refused steadily to let him interrupt her conversation. The poor little fellow tried for nearly an hour to get her attention, and then wet his pants and got into trouble. Another situation is when every two words are interrupted by a child or children who have no regard for the parents or other adults at all. It's very disrespectful. What's the answer, well there is happy medium. Teach the children not to interrupt unless its important and then teach them to let the adult speaking, finish the sentence. Teach them always to say, "Excuse me" just as you would yourself. When it's possible and at certain points in the conversation, include the children. That way they will learn to be respectful of adults and but at the same time not ignored and made to feel like they are a pain to everyone.

"Dear Father,

Thank you for this Thanksgiving dinner. There will be a lot left over which I would be happy to send to Africa, but by the time they get it, it might go bad, but thank you anyway and please take care of those poor children." Lisa, age 7.

From "Fact or Fantasy" *childrens bible study*

Chapter Ten

Children and the Spiritual Realm

Children and Intercession

I have been covering a few negative things these last few chapters so now I want to dwell on the inheritance our kids have in the Lord. Since this is my husband, David's main ministry, I now get to preach a little of his vision (and mine) for the children.

It is very hard for children to relate to God if He is presented to them second hand. Often they think that He's **your** God. They have to know God for themselves so that He becomes a personal friend. God loves to reveal Himself to children. He is willing to manifest His presence to them in awesome ways. In our ministry we have seen both young and older kids overwhelmed with the Holy Spirit, being transfixed, (like the 19th century evangelist Maria Woodworth-Etter), healed, delivered, used in true intercession, with weeping. We have also witnessed them used by the Lord in healing and miracles. We have known of a couple of people get out of wheel-chairs through the ministry of the children, and many deaf people healed. God will speak to them in a wonderful way, if they are taught to listen.

I will give you some examples:- One day when Faith was about only ten or eleven years old she came to me. "I don't understand mama, I keep getting a pain in my chest." I didn't sense it was anything physical, and I prayed with her about it. As we prayed, Faith had a vision of a man who had recently visited at our home. His name was Ron and he always wore Tee-shirts with scriptures written on the front. "I believe it is something to do with this man," Faith said. We prayed for him in the Spirit, as we didn't know what to pray in the natural realm. A couple of days later, we were driving somewhere and Faith spoke up. "I have that pain again, we need to pray for the man with the Tee shirt." The following Saturday, Faith and I were walking across the parking lot of the local mall. She stopped and said, "Oh, we must pray for the man again." We stood right there and prayed. When we finally arrived home, I called Ron to see what was happening in his life. I didn't tell him about the word of knowledge Faith had about him. Ron was excited, he was an architect and builder, he built large expensive houses. "Well," Ron explained, "I built three houses and have been paying the mortgage on all of them. I couldn't seem to sell them. Last year I had a serious heart attack, and my doctor told me that I would be in real trouble if I had any more stress. This week, I was under so much pressure over the houses, and several times I began to have pains across my chest." Ron began talking fast, "I was fearful, I thought I was going to go "home" any minute, but you know, today I had another pain, and suddenly it was as if a weight was lifted off my chest, and I know I was healed. Not only that but I received an impartation of faith to sell these houses, and they are now all under contracts." Ron laughed. I told him that my little girl was praying for him.

During "Desert Storm," the Lord gave Faith a mini-movie vision of an American pilot, shot down in the desert. She saw him looking for somewhere to hide and she prayed. She saw in her spirit, a plane coming from the American base searching for him. Faith prayed again for the pilot to be found. The search plane flew on a few extra miles and guess what? They found that pilot. The account of the pilot's testimony was later written in a 1991 "Readers Digest." At other times both Lisa and Faith have had words of knowledge for major ministries..."*God is no respecter of persons.*" (**Acts.10:34**).

Children and the Supernatural

Children are very open to the supernatural, they also have an in-built awareness that there is "something else" apart from the realm that they can see and hear with their natural eyes and ears. That is why they are often drawn to science-fiction and even occult type movies. It is very important that they can see that God is a God of the supernatural realm. The things of the Spirit, heaven, angels etc. are all a part of our (and their) inheritance, so it should be a part of our lives. *(See __Living in the Supernatural__ by Kathie Walters)*. I have believed for both of our girls that God will manifest Himself to them personally. Both Faith and Lisa's salvation experience was supernatural. Two angels took Faith to heaven, she met Jesus and came back baptized in the Holy Spirit and speaking in other tongues. Lisa also had an experience directly with the Holy Spirit.

When Faith was attending school, she would wake up early. She liked to listen to her Amy Grant tapes, before getting out of bed. I would put one in her tape player for her, but if the volume was too loud or too soft, she would fall asleep again. One morning I put a tape in, and I forgot to turn up the volume, she started to fall back to sleep, but suddenly the volume was turned up for about a minute, enough to wake her up, and then it was turned down again. There was no one that she could see in the room. The very next day she had a similar experience. This time though, the tape had played all the way through and Faith was drifting off to sleep. Someone ejected the tape, turned it over, placed it back into the recorder, and pushed down the "play" button. I had a friend staying overnight in the bedroom next door to Faith, she told me that her door opened and although she didn't see anyone, the room was filled with a wonderful presence and sweet perfume. The same angel who had ministered to Faith, paid my girlfriend a visit also.

There are many stories I could tell you about the realm of the supernatural and children. The point is that God desires our children to have more than mere head-knowledge and religious information.

Children and Deliverance

We have prayed for many children for deliverance from demonic activity. To suggest to some parents that their little children may need deliverance is like telling them that their children have fleas. Unfortunately, demonic activity can be passed down through generations. As Christians we have the power to break these strongholds in the Name of Jesus. I have known children to have spirits of anger, hatred, fear, infirmity, religion etc. The Holy Spirit will show you if you seek His counsel. He will tell you what to pray. My grandfather was a Freemason and because of this involvement I was delivered from several spirits that came down through my family tree. Death, infirmity, sorcery, false brotherhood, false loyalty and false light. These are the main strongholds that had to be broken over my life. Divination (fortune telling), occult involvement, cult participation, all need to be broken off in the spirit if you or any member of your family has been involved in it, even to the third and fourth generation. Children are affected by television, music, movies and cartoons, that can have undertones of demonic activity. There are spirits behind some of these things. If a child is prone to certain behavior patterns, temper, resentment, anger, moodiness, misery, heaviness etc. he or she probably needs deliverance. I recommend a book, Deliverance for Children and Teens by Bill Banks, if you feel that you would like to know more about this subject. It may be ordered from our ministry.

Christians cannot be demon possessed, but they can posses demons. The good news is that Jesus is our **Deliverer.** While God has made provision for our total well-being, nothing is **automatic.** Salvation is available, but it doesn't just happen, you have to **receive** it to be saved. Healing is available for every area of our lives, be it physical, emotional, financial, but it is not automatic, you have to **receive** it. Deliverance is available but like everything else, you have to avail yourself of it. **(See Deut.18:9-13. Deut.28. Ex**

47

20:5, 34:7. Num 14:18). If we serve the Lord in our lifetime, then the blessings will also come upon our children.

"Dear God,

Please help my Grandma to save my Grandpa. He is grouchy and he needs your Gospel very much to make him happy and nice and go to heaven." Barry, age 6.

Chapter Eleven

Children and "Church"

David and I have been in some churches and have had a wonderful move of God upon the children. Sometimes a mother will come to us at the end of a service and say, "I wish my son (or daughter) had been here. We ask, "Why weren't they?" "Oh, they didn't want to come, they wanted to go to the mall with their friends." Or something similar comes forth. We then ask, "How old is your son/daughter?" The answer sometimes is, "Nine" or "twelve" or "fifteen." "You mean, they have a choice?," We ask. Some parents have a funny sense of authority. They think that if they make their kids come to church, they will hate God and hate the church. We usually explain it to them this way. "On Monday then do you ask them if they would like to go to school?" Do you give them a choice whether they would like to take a shower, or change their underwear? Do you think that if you make them brush their teeth thcy will come to hate toothbrushes or have an emotional war with soap for the rest of their lives? Of course not, it's not a valid argument. *"Train up a child in the way he should go and when he is old he will not depart from it."* **(Prov.22:6).** Another, understanding of "old" is **independent.** While a child is under your roof and dependant upon you for food and shelter etc. He or she is also under your authority. You do not have to make this a heavy thing. You can keep your authority and still stay lighthearted. If you have authority in the Spirit you can say something strong, in a light way, even with a smile, without having a big heavy cloud over you. The point is that your decisions are **not** open for discussion.

Sometimes a parent has asked us this question after a seminar. "My son is fifteen he is nearly six foot tall. I have allowed him to goof off and not made him come to church with the rest of the family because he didn't want to. I see that is wrong, but how do I now go to this huge person who is used to doing his own thing and make him come with us and be a part of what we are doing." David tells them this, "Go back to your teenager and ask them for forgiveness, tell them you have allowed them to do their own thing, because either you were intimidated by them and just wanted peace and quiet at any price. Or in some way you thought you were helping them. Explain that God has shown you that to allow them to just go their own way and do their own thing can only bring them trouble. The devil loves it. Say that from now on you are going to protect them and care for them spiritually as well as physically, and from this time they will come with the rest of the family to church and begin to get involved. Tell them that you love them too much to allow them to become Satan's property. Remember God has a destiny for their lives. Keep reminding them of that."

Dad, don't allow your children to talk back, or have a bad attitude toward their mother. Teach them to respect her. Evelyn Hamon says that her four children, who by the way are all in full time ministry now, were not allowed under any circumstances to have a disrespectful attitude, **in word, look or manner**. An excellent tape of Evelyn Hamon, <u>Training your Child</u> can be ordered from our ministry.

Have you seen children during church service just goofing around, falling asleep, coloring under the chair? Explain to them what church is all about. It's good to start by telling them what church **isn't**. It's not a playground, or a race track, or a bedroom to go to sleep. It's where they come to worship the Lord, and be equipped to become mighty for God. I have been in several churches lately and heard a small child talk and chatter throughout the service uncorrected. That is encouraging a child to think that it's alright for them to do their own thing, even in the meeting. Teach them to participate and sit still and listen. Do you know the Holy Spirit holds you responsible for your child's behavior. Remember Eli, the Priest. The judgment of God came upon him, because he did not discipline his sons. God spoke to Samuel of Eli and said, *"I will judge his house forever for the iniquity that he knows, because his sons made themselves vile and **he did not restrain them."** (1 Sam.3:13).* Remember Samuel himself was but a boy **(v 1).**

In our church in England, there were several couples with small babies. One couple got into a habit of holding the baby in such a way that it got the attention of everyone around them. Instead of worshipping or listening to the Word that was coming forth, the people around played with the baby. They allowed the baby to take the attention away from the Lord Jesus. The Holy Spirit spoke to me and told me that if they didn't stop it, the grace of God would not be on the family. Do you realize that His grace keeps us from all kinds of troubles? He told me the family would come under attack and the umbrella of grace would not be there to protect them. Sure enough a week later the baby was in the hospital, sick. You see the whole issue was pride, it came out in how they behaved with the baby. God resists our pride, **(see Jas.4:5).** It is a sickening thing to Him. The couple saw what they were doing, repented and God's grace was restored. Maybe this is hard for you to swallow, but I have known this to happen on several occasions. The Holy Spirit will not compete for our attention and affection. We must learn to reverence and honor Him, and teach our children also.

At another meeting there was a beautiful anointing present. A little boy was throwing toys all over the place and causing a disturbance, trying to get attention. The parents did nothing about it, they seemed to think it was "cute." Suddenly I felt the anointing lift and the place suddenly seemed empty. "Why are you leaving?" I asked the Holy Spirit. He answered, "I will not share My glory with...." We must be careful with God's presence. Sometimes we have been praying for people and the glory of the Lord is present. At the back of the auditorium, there are people walking about, chatting, and children playing and running around. We are not teaching them a reverence for God. Pastors, parents, keep the youngsters in order, teach them to love and give honor in the Presence of the Lord. Remember when children and teens attend school they are required to study and be involved in the program, attending only is not enough. What teacher would allow kid's to sit in class and play with their fingers, or just talk to each other? Attending church is also not enough, they must enter in and participate.

Ask your Pastor to make a point of making reference to the children in his message, tell them, "This is for you, you're **not** too young to listen and hear from God." You will amazed what a difference it will make. David, when he preaches, always makes eye contact with the children and speaks directly to them. Often because they are ignored, the children think the service is not really for them because it's Mom and Dad's church. They assume that "important" people like the pastor, have little regard for them. Remember they are the church too. I have heard some pastors say, "God hasn't called me to minister to children." Well I really question that statement. Not to be offensive, but if the "Great Shepherd" felt called to minister to the children surely the under-shepherds should not have a different calling. If a Pastor or shepherd is called to minister to a particular Body, or Church, that must include the younger saints. They are a part, they are**not** the church of tomorrow, as I hear so often, they are the **Church of today and the leaders of tomorrow.**

Phil Phillips (Turmoil in the Toy Box) related to David of a service he had attended where children were going forward to respond to an altar call and then were told by the deacons to return to their seats, because they were too young to understand. He also tells of a situation where a fourteen year old responded to an altar call and the pastor prayed over the youth, "Father we thank you for this boy being here. We pray that when he is older, he can make a quality decision for you." How tragic that many adults have that mentality. When kids understand that they are a real part of the Body of Christ, teach them to join in the worship. I taught my children at home. We had "meetings" we would read the Bible and sing and worship. When we sang, we **all** stood and raised out hands and danced. I showed them in the scriptures where it said how to worship, raising hands and clapping, etc. Train them to raise their hands and enter in. If my children caused a problem fidgeting in church, we had practice all week. Every day we practiced sitting still for a while. They soon learned! If they play up in the meeting, take them outside, discipline them and bring them back. Don't give up and take them to the nursery to play. They will soon learn that if they play up enough, you will get fed up and take them out. Then they have won and you have lost. Teach them to listen to the message and give them a note book to write down a few things that catch their attention. I didn't allow my girls to draw pictures instead. They did at first and then I caught on to them. They told me that the pictures were to do with the message, but I couldn't understand what aeroplane, kites and cats had to do with the "Fruit of the Spirit!" I didn't allow dolls, bears, crayons and coloring books. The devil will make sure that those things get their attention off what is going on. They are purely a distraction, and you are teaching them to "switch off." It's much easier to let the kids goof off, and then the parents don't have to work to train them how to behave. The end result is worth the effort work with them.

The media and so called psychology, has given us the impression that children can't be expected to sit still and give their attention to something for more than ten minutes. Well, we've been brain washed. Of course they can. Put a child in front of a video game and see how long it can keep their attention. David tells the children in our services, "You really, really, can sit still, you will not die!" they **do** sit still. I could go on explaining the children's place in the church, bringing them into Spiritual gifts, and exposing them to the anointing. That can all be found in David's book *Equipping the Younger Saints.*

"Dear Father God,
*   I know you made EVERYTHING. I don't know how you do it and have time to listen to all the kids in the world, but I know you do." Kelly, age 7.*

From "Being A Christian" *children bible study*

— Chapter Twelve—

Allowing Them to Choose

Enjoy your children, if they are disciplined they will be a delight to you and will add wonderful joyous portions to your life. Take time to do what **they** want to do sometimes. Even if it's not "your cup of tea." Learn to take an interest and **listen.** As they mature, their tastes regarding clothes, dress styles, and music become defined. Don't just toss everything out of the window because it's not your taste. (I don't mean that you should put up with stuff you know is harmful to their spirit). I kept buying clothes for Faith and Lisa, that **I liked**. I thought they looked great in the things I bought for them. A lot of that stuff hung in the closet and was never worn, unless they were staying home. They only did that to make me happy. I would tell them they were being wasteful. I began to realize gradually that it was pointless trying to make them adopt my tastes. Actually they have very good taste, I even began to like their music. (No heavy rock) I found that they always checked the groups whose music they played. They would listen to the reported interviews. They found out the kind of testimony they had. If it turned out to be poor, they would not listen to the music, nor watch the videos. The Lord had put His standards within them, for which I am very grateful. You see there was a transition, from my disciplines to that inward discipline that comes from the Holy Spirit. I was gradually able to let them make their own choices in many instances. Sometimes I feel overawed by the wisdom God has deposited in Faith. She often ministers to me.

56

It is very hard for a young person to come under the authority and discipline of the Lord, if he or she has never come under the authority and discipline of their parents. It can take years and years to learn to submit to the Spirit. It isn't a loving thing to allow a child to "do his own thing." *"Therefore the law was our tutor to bring us to Christ, that we might be justified by faith. After faith has come, we are no longer under a tutor."* **(Gal.3:24-25).**

If you have more than one child make sure you take special time for each. Dad, from time to time take your daughter out on a "dinner date." Then buy her a pretty, new dress. You can be her beau until she meets Mr. Right. She doesn't have to date around to find somebody. God already has someone just right for her. She only needs that one special person. It is unnecessary for her to have numerous boyfriends to try out. Those situations can tend to mess up her emotions. Also, it's the way of the world. Encourage your son to wait for the Lord to send him his princess. Encourage him to look to the Lord and WAIT for the special young lady. One who is virtuous, one who really loves Jesus. Some girls just look for boyfriends to build up their own ego.

Sometimes you can select a person in your household, one of the kids, or Mom or Dad and have a special day for them. Sometimes we have a "Faith" day or a "Lisa" day. Everyone else spoils that person all day long. I take them out and buy a couple of frivolous things. God does that you know. He doesn't want us to be led by the lust of the eye, to want everything we take a fancy to. He does shower us with special little gifts just to let us know that He intimately cares.

One year, I asked the Lord if He was going to give me a birthday present as He had done on previous occasions. He replied, "Yes, what would you like to have?" I gave it some thought and decided that I would really like some "Joy" perfume. I thought maybe it was a little extravagant. So I asked the Holy Spirit if it was alright to ask for that? I waited for the answer. During a Bible study that morning an Evangelist was teaching from the scripture. He looked up suddenly and said, "You shall have joy always." I can't remember the context, but the words flew out of his mouth and hit me. "Thank you Lord," I said silently. When I returned home I made soup and a sandwich for the people at my house. The Evangelist who was visiting, spoke to me as he was leaving, "The Lord impressed me to give you some **cold cash** to buy a present, so I have put it in the **refrigerator**." I went to the **"fridge"** and guess what was sitting there on a plate? It was exactly the right amount of money for the perfume. God is wonderful. He also has a sense of humor.

God wants you to believe Him to move on your children. As you release your faith, His Spirit will deal with them. He sometimes will tell you what to do, sometimes He will do it Himself. It's great. Once, David and I were driving somewhere. We had to take the girls with us. They really didn't want to come, especially Lisa. She began to complain. She went on and on. She just wouldn't quit. Finally, I turned around and said, "Lisa, if you don't stop complaining, the Holy Spirit will deal with you." But she was on a roll, she carried on, then suddenly she became very quiet. I looked around again, her eyes were as big as saucers and her mouth was open. "What is it?" I asked. "There is a hand on my tummy and it's being squashed." "Well you should stop whining and start praising the Lord, or the angel will keep his hand there," I told her. She began quietly to tell the Lord she was sorry and she began to praise Him. After a few minutes, she began to smile. The hand had lifted off her tummy. There were other occasions when the same thing happened to her. She knew she wasn't just dealing with me. Boy, what a difference it makes.

One little boy in one of our meetings, was goofing around, saying stupid things. God struck him dumb, or to put it nicely, took His voice away. The little guy was unable to make a sound. His mouth was opening and shutting like a goldfish. He looked very comical. After a while he got down on his knees and repented for the things he had said. God immediately gave him his voice back. If you believe, God will minister to your children. Sometimes the Holy Spirit has pinned small children to the floor, until they have "straightened up" their attitudes, in a meeting.

God loves to show the children that He is real, and He delights to show them that He cares about their relationship with Him. After all it's His army we are raising, He is the Great General, He will take care of His troops. He also is the Great Shepherd, He will tend His sheep, even the little ones.

SINGLE PARENTS AND DIVORCEE'S

There are situation's where children are shared between parents who are separated or divorced. For example there may be a Christian Mom who has a son and every other weekend he spends with his dad. His mother takes him to church and attempts to raise him to live by Christian principles, but when he goes to be with dad he enters a non-christian environment. Alcohol, smoking, bad language R or X rated video's. Little Johnny wants to be like his dad. His dad is his hero. The boy has conflicts. What is the solution? It is important that the son has a real salvation experience and not just a nominal Christian upbringing. It is also important that he understands that his dad is lost. He must be shown that when he goes to see his dad, God is sending him as a witness and a missionary. He must tell his dad that although he loves him, he can't watch the videos and be around the bad language etc. He would be willing to pray for him and he would like his dad to take him to church. The father may fuss at first and mutter things about the poor boy being brainwashed with religious junk. The child must show real genuine concern about his dad's spiritual condition. If the child's own relationship with the Lord is real and strong you will be amazed what God can do. Many children have led their parents to the Lord.

One little boy who was ten at the time was in one of David's workshops and the Lord spoke to him about witnessing to his friends at his school and in his neighborhood. In two years he has led over 100 children to the Lord. Another little boy who was saved in an evangelistic crusade, asked for prayer. He did not want to go back home, because his mother was a drunk and his dad beat him. He also had to take care of his seven brother and sisters. The evangelist prayed for him and encouraged him to go back home as God's missionary. Over the next six evenings the boy return with one or two of his brothers and sisters until they all had received the Lord. Then toward the end he brought his mother. Finally on the last night their father joined them. The whole family found the Lord. *"A little child shall lead them."* **(Isa.11:6)**.

NOTE

I know there are many people that have extenuating circumstances and their families need specialized counseling. I am not trying to cover every situation. This booklet is merely to offer a few guidelines, to help with the most common problems that I see in the average Christian family. It is really simple, it's realizing that you as a parent can have spiritual authority, and that makes all the difference to your household and to yourself. This younger generation are the ones going to be used greatly to gather in the harvest. They are going to be sent to every Nation. They are going to demonstrate the power of God in a way that we have not seen before. That is why it is important that our children are raised, not just with religious head-knowledge, but with an experience of God. An anointed and appointed army of young warriors, ready to go into all the world.

Other Books Available Through
GOOD NEWS MINISTRIES
by Kathie Walters

Angels Watching over You - Did you know that Angels are very active in our everyday lives?

The Bright and Shining Revival - An account of the Hebrides Revival 1948 - 1952 The praying men and women of the Hebrides clung to the promise that if they sought Him, He would Heal Their Land.

Celtic Flames - Read the exciting accounts of famous fourth- and fifth century Celtic Christians: Patrick, Brendan, Cuthbert, Brigid and others.

Columba - The Celtic Dove - Read about the prophetic and miraculous ministry of this famous Celtic Christian, filled with supernatural visitations.

Elitism & the False Shepherding Spirit This book discusses Control, Manipulation, False Shepherding Spirit, Spirit of Abortion, Grief and how to be set free from them.

Living in the Supernatural - Kathie believes that the supernatural realm, the angels, miracles, and signs and wonders are the spiritual inheritance: of every believer, as in the early church. She tells how to embrace and enter into our inheritance.

The Spirit of False Judgment - Dealing with heresy hunters. Sometimes things are different from what we perceive them to be.

The Visitation - An account of two visitations from the Lord that Kathie experienced. One lasted for seven days and the other for three and one half weeks. An account also of a visitation her daughter Faith had when she was just 17 years old.

Seer's List And Health Related Mindsets - Explanation of the Seer anointing and how it "works." and, Part 2 - Various mindsets the Lord has shown me that can bring sickness.

**Kathie Walters speaks and ministers in the anointing
at churches and women's conferences.**

For further information or
order forms, please call or write:
Good News Fellowship Ministries
220 Sleepy Creek Road
Macon, Georgia 31210
Phone (478) 757-8071 - Fax (478) 757-0136
E-mail: goodnews@reynoldscable.net
http://www.goodnews.netministries.org

by David Walters

Kids in Combat - David shows how to train children and teens in spiritual power and bring them into the anointing for ministry (parents, teachers and children/youth pastors).

Equipping the Younger Saints - Teaching children and youth the baptism of the Holy Spirit and spiritual gifts (parents, teachers, children, youth pastors).

Children Aflame - Amazing accounts of children from the journals of the great Methodist preacher John Wesley in the 1700's and David's own accounts with children and youth.

The Anointing and You - What we must do to receive, sustain, impart, and channel the anointing for renewal/revival, and to pass it on to the younger generation.

Worship fur Dummies - David Walters calls himself a dummy in the area of praise and worship, but he knows the ways of the Holy Spirit.

Radical Living in an Ungodly Society - Our ungodly Society really targets our children and youth. How do we cope with this situation.

Children's Bible Study Books

Armor of God – Children's illustrated Bible study on Ephesians 6:14-18 (ages 6-14 years).

Fruit of the Spirit – Children's illustrated Bible study on Galatians 5:22 (ages 6-14 years).

Fact or Fantasy – Children's illustrated Bible study on Christian apologetics. How to defend your faith (ages 8-15 years).

Being a Christian – Children's illustrated Bible study on what it really means to be a Christian (ages 7-14 years).

Children's Prayer Manual – Children's illustrated study on prayer (ages 6-14 years).

Available in Spring 2004

Gifts of the Spirit – *Children's* illustrated Bible study on the Gifts of the Spirit (ages 6-14 years).

**For further information or
order forms, please call or write:
Good News Fellowship Ministries
220 Sleepy Creek Road
Macon, Georgia 31210
Phone (478) 757-8071 - Fax (478) 757-0136
E-mail: goodnews@reynoldscable.net
http://www.goodnews.netministries.org**